THESE ARE OUR BODIES

FOR PRIMARY

Church Publishing
NEW YORK

PARENT BOOK

Scripture from the *New Revised Standard Version Bible (NRSV)* © 1989 by the Division of Christian Education of the National Council of Churches of Christ in the USA. Used by permission.

Scripture quotations from the CEB used with permission. All rights reserved. Common English Bible, Copyright 2011.

A catalog record of this book is available from the Library of Congress.

Church Publishing Incorporated
19 East 34th Street
New York, NY 10016

Cover design by: Jennifer Kopec, 2 Pug Design
Typeset by: Progressive Publishing Services

ISBN-13: 978-0-89869-015-6 (pbk.)
ISBN-13: 978-0-89869-023-1 (ebook)

Printed in the United States of America

CONTENTS

INTRODUCTION

Welcome to *These Are Our Bodies*!

Then God said, "Let us make humanity in our image to resemble us so that they may take charge of the fish of the sea, the birds in the sky, the livestock, all the earth, and all the crawling things on earth. God created humanity in God's own image, in the divine image God created them, male and female God created them. God saw everything he had made: it was supremely good."

—Genesis 1:26–27, 31 (CEB)

As children of God we are born into the world beloved by God. We come into the world inherently worthy of love and awe— awe at the mystery of our holiness in who and what we are. As children develop, their experience and sense of self are shaped and molded by those around them. This includes sexuality.

In these primary sessions, you are invited to explore the concepts of faith, creation, empowerment, and acceptance with your child and with other parents.

As a parent,[1] you began teaching your child about bodies from the first moment that you held your child. In the next few sessions we want to encourage you, as a parent, to intentionally consider the lessons you are teaching your child as they grow and learn more about the world around them.

This Parent Book is for you—for you to ponder and journal thoughts, insights and your reflections. Our hope is that you will enjoy this journey with your young child.

Jenny Beaumont and Abbi Long

....

1 We recognize and celebrate that families are unique! We use the term "parents" to refer to anyone who is raising children. These resources and the parent sessions are designed for use by grandparents, relatives, teachers, or friends who are raising children.

SESSION 1

GOD
KNOWS ME

The gatekeeper opens the gate for him,
and the sheep hear his voice.
He calls his own sheep by name and leads them out.
I am the good shepherd.
I know my own and my own know me,
just as the Father knows me and I know the Father.
—John 10:3, 14–15

In the Session

Thank you God for keeping me near to you and for caring for me. I know that you love my family and me. Help me to learn more about you and the special way that you created all of me. *Amen*.

On Your Own

In this session, you were invited to consider how it felt to be sheep in Jesus' flock. The children learned:

- Jesus told them about sheep and shepherds. Jesus said that he was like a shepherd and that his sheep knew the sound of his voice. And Jesus said that he knew each of his sheep. Jesus said that he takes care of all of his sheep.

- Jesus said that we were like sheep.

How does it feel for Jesus to know you?

How does it feel for Jesus to know your name?

In the session, you and your child made a STORY OF ME book. What warmed your heart to remember?

What was the best part to share with your child?

What was your beginning?

What is the story of your name?

Describe your gift from God.

What is the story of your baptism?

What is your story now?

A Blessing

The LORD bless you and keep you;
the LORD make his face to shine upon you,
and be gracious to you
the LORD lift up his countenance upon you,
and give you peace.[2]

2 Numbers 6:24–26.

With Your Family at Home

You may want to use this activity later to complete this portion of your child's Participant Book, found on page 15.

The story of the Good Shepherd helps us remember that God knows us by name. Use the sheep below to think about the parable again from John 10.

Can you give them each a name?

Whom else does God know by name in your family?

What are the names of some friends that God knows by name?

With crayons or markers, add to the pictures of the sheep. Draw some grass or ground. Add in the sky. Write "Jesus knows us by name."

SESSION 2

I AM
LOVED

"I give you a new commandment: Love each other.
Just as I have loved you, so you also must love each other.
This is how everyone will know that you are my disciples,
when you love each other."
—John 13:34–35 (CEB)

Dear God, thank you for loving me and for sending Jesus and giving us a new commandment: To love each other, as you have loved us. Help me to love my friends and myself, too. *Amen*.

In the Session

In the session, we learned that a blessing is like a prayer, a hopeful prayer that inspires and lifts people.

People were bringing little children to him in order that he might touch them and bless them. The disciples tried to shoo them away. But when Jesus saw this, he was upset and said to them, "Don't you dare try to keep these little ones from me. Let me hold them. The Kingdom of God belongs to little ones just like these. If you aren't open to God's kingdom like a little child is open, you will never enter the kingdom." And he picked them up in his arms and laid his hands on the children and blessed them.

—Mark 10: 13–16[3]

What do we learn about Jesus from this story?

3 Lyn Zill Briggs. *God's Word, My Voice; A Lectionary for Children* (New York: Church Publishing, 2016), 347. Used by permission.

What do we learn about ourselves?

BLESSINGS

Make a blessing prayer for your child. Your child can help color and decorate the prayer. The words or drawings represent or describe the attribute(s) of your child.

Some examples include the following:

loving	hopeful	smart
kind	grateful	selfless
gentle	enthusiastic	faithful
prayerful	joyful	
generous	thoughtful	

Write some of your own words or descriptions below.

On Your Own

This week, as you go out into the world, bless your child.

_____ is _____,
_____, and _____. Thank
you God for _____.

> Loving and awesome God, thank you for my family. Thank you for giving me people to love and people who love me. Help us to remember that we have all been blessed by your grace. Stay close to us and keep us close to each other as we learn and grow. *Amen.*

Write your own prayer of thankfulness for your child.

With Your Family at Home

You may want to use this activity later to complete this portion of your child's Participant Book, found on page 25.

The story of Jesus and the little children reminds us that Jesus loved all people, even very young people. He welcomed them with his hands wide open. Trace both of your hands. You can also trace your parents' hands on top of your hands. Use a different color crayon or marker so you can see the different hands.

Then draw the faces or bodies of all the people you think Jesus welcomes. You can draw yourself. You can draw your friends at church or school. You can draw other children and people in the world. Write below your picture: Jesus Welcomes Everyone!

Prayer

Loving and awesome God, thank you for my family. Thank you for giving me people to love and people who love me. Help us to remember that we have all been blessed by your grace. Stay close to us and keep us close to each other as we learn and grow. *Amen*.

GOD
MADE ME

O Lord, you have searched me and known me.
You know when I sit down and when I rise up;
you discern my thoughts from far away.
You search out my path and my lying down,
and are acquainted with all my ways.
Even before a word is on my tongue,
O Lord, you know it completely.
You hem me in, behind and before,
and lay your hand upon me.
even the darkness is not dark to you;
the night is as bright as the day,
for darkness is as light to you.

For it was you who formed my inward parts;
you knit me together in my mother's womb.
I praise you, for I am fearfully and wonderfully made.
Wonderful are your works;

that I know very well.
My frame was not hidden from you,
when I was being made in secret,
intricately woven in the depths of the earth.
Your eyes beheld my unformed substance.
In your book were written
all the days that were formed for me,
when none of them as yet existed.
How weighty to me are your thoughts, O God!
How vast is the sum of them!
—Psalm 139:1–5, 12–17

In the Session

Thank you, God, for always being with me. God looks for me and finds me. God leads me to places to play and keep me safe. God knows even when I stand up and when I sit down again. When I look around, I see what God has created. Help me to be still and know God is the Lord. *Amen*.[4]

In this session, your child learned about these messages:
- God created each of us, and we are wonderful.
- We all have bodies and we all have a body that is one of a kind.
- Our bodies are always changing and growing.

What are some of your reflections on Psalm 139? Take time to journal about your insights.

....

4 Adapted from Psalm 46 and Psalm 139.

Young children can be challenged by thinking about gifts or talents. Asking them to brainstorm things that they enjoy doing is easier for them. Our gifts are tied to what we love doing.

I am grateful for . . .

Think about the amazing things that your body can do and the things you love to do. Write down something about your body you are grateful for, and write down why you are grateful.

I thank God for all of these children who are perfectly and uniquely made.

I am grateful for _____ because _____.

Thank you, Creator God, who made me—all of me—inside and out!

On Your Own

"Telling children how babies come into the world is a story of love and belonging that includes biology, family structure, and faith. Yes, it is a story about the human body, people, sperm, and eggs; it is also a story of God's beautiful creation. It is a story of faith, hope, and love—a story of God working in our lives. Who would want to miss that?"[5]

> For the Lord is a great God, and a great King above all gods. In his hand are all the corners of the earth, and the strength of the hills is his also. The sea is his and he made it, and his hands prepared the dry land.[6]
> —Psalm 95:3–5

As children of God we are born into the world beloved by God. We come into the world inherently worthy of love and awe— awe at the mystery of our holiness in who and what we are. As children develop, their experience and sense of self are shaped and molded by those around them. This includes sexuality. It is inherently part of who we are; living as a sexual being is unavoidable and unavoidably complex. Sexuality is good—a gift from God since the beginning.

....

5 Leslie Choplin and Jenny Beaumont. *These Are Our Bodies: Talking Faith and Sexuality at Church & at Home Foundation Book* (New York: Church Publishing, 2016), page 196.

6 Book of Common Prayer, 44

Then God said, "Let us make humanity in our image to resemble us so that they may take charge of the fish of the sea, the birds in the sky, the livestock, all the earth, and all the crawling things on earth. God created humanity in God's own image, in the divine image God created them, male and female God created them. God saw everything he had made: it was supremely good."

—Genesis 1:26–27, 31

Parents begin teaching their children about their bodies from the first moment that they hold their children. In the next few sessions, we want to encourage you, as a parent, to intentionally consider the lessons you are teaching your children as you hold, feed, and tickle them. And to choose ways of speaking, acting and touching that show your young children that they are created and loved by God—body and all.

With Your Family at Home

You may want to use this activity later to complete this portion of your child's Participant Book, found on page 35.

Psalm 139 reminds us that God made us—inside and out. It reminds us that God knows about our lives; even things we think are a secret. Talk about the game "Hide and Go Seek." What are the rules to the game? Write down those rules here (in your child's book).

Draw three places you might hide in a game of "Hide and Seek."

Can you hide from God? Can you go somewhere that God's love cannot reach? Talk about hiding from God or God's love with your family. Why might we try to hide from God's love? Will God come and seek us if we try to hide?

Circle an answer for each of these questions. Talk about your answers together.

1. Is there anything we can do to make God love us less?

   Yes   No   I don't know

2. Is there anything we can say to make God love us less?

   Yes   No   I don't know

3. Is there anywhere we can go where God's love won't seek us out?

   Yes   No   I don't know

Thank you, Creator God, who made me—all of me—inside and out!

WE ARE
EMPOWERED

Love is patient; love is kind; love is not envious or boastful or
arrogant or rude. It does not insist on its own way; it is not
irritable or resentful; it does not rejoice in wrongdoing, but
rejoices in the truth. It bears all things, believes all things,
hopes all things, endures all things. And now faith, hope, and
love abide, these three; and the greatest of these is love.

—1 Corinthians 13:4–7, 13

Almighty God, giver of good gifts, we thank you for these
parents. We are grateful for their faithfulness and their
steadfast hand as they guide, teach and love the children
within their care. Give them the wisdom to follow your will
and pass along the gifts they have been given; through
Jesus Christ our Lord. *Amen*.

In the Session

Faith connections are uncomplicated to use because they reflect your faith and your experience with God. They are personal, yet simple. "No matter what happens, I love you and God loves you." "There is nothing that we can ever do that will separate us from God's love." "You are uniquely and wonderfully made!"

Faith connections express our deepest truths about faith and ourselves in the context of our everyday lives. They are simple, and even with our primary age children, are uncomplicated. They are the foundation for what we do and say.

How do you express faith connections and help your child internalize those values? How do you decide which faith connections to teach?

STEP ONE:

Begin by thinking about your own foundational values—the words that help you in difficult situations. Think about the values that your child needs in order to live a faith-filled life. If you only had five things to teach your child, what would you choose?

STEP TWO:

Keep a list of faith connections to impart to your children. Work with a parenting partner or friend to choose some values that resonate with your family.

STEP THREE:

Check them off as you hear your child expresses those values in conversations with you. Once they have internalized the value, check it off the list. Then move on to the next value to be learned.

STEP FOUR:

Be patient with yourself. Remember you are creating the framework for your child from which their values, especially values about their identity, will spring. Creating value statements takes practice. Try a few value statements and remember to adjust them over time as you continue the conversations with your child.

Here are a few examples of faith connections that we have shared with parents, and that parents have shared with us, over the years:

- God loves you; that means all of you. Your spirit and your body are beautiful.

- God made a way for families to have babies. Our bodies are perfectly created to make babies.

- God made each of us uniquely different and wonderful. We are made in the image of God.[7]

What are the values about God and bodies that are most important to you?

What messages would have been helpful to you growing up?

....

7 Leslie Choplin and Jenny Beaumont. *These Are Our Bodies: Talking Faith & Sexuality at Church & Home Foundation Book* (New York: Church Publishing, 2016). Read more in Chapter 25, "A Framework to Answer Questions" in this book.

What values or faith connections do you want to make with your growing child?

On Your Own

Homework for next session: read chapter 24, "When to Begin the Conversation" in *These Are Our Bodies: Foundation Book*. We will discuss this in our next session.

> Almighty God, we are grateful for your immeasurable love and for the love of parents and children. Help us to let your love shine through us to all those children who are watching us. Let us love you with a whole heart, focused on you and bathed in grace. In Christ Name we pray. *Amen*.

With Your Family at Home

You may want to use this activity later to complete this portion of your child's Participant Book, found on pages 39–40.

Together as a family, fill in these blanks with your own words.

God loves _____; that means all of _____. Your spirit and your body are _____.

God made a way for families to have _____. Our bodies are perfectly created to make _____.

God made each of us unique individuals and _____. We are made in the image of _____.

Write your own family's faith connections here:

WE CONTINUE THE CONVERSATION

You shall put these words of mine in your heart and soul, and you shall bind them as a sign on your hand, and fix them as an emblem on your forehead. Teach them to your children, talking about them when you are at home and when you are away, when you lie down and when you rise. Write them on the doorposts of your house and on your gates, so that your days and the days of your children may be multiplied in the land that the Lord swore to your ancestors to give them, as long as the heavens are above the earth.

—Deuteronomy 11:18–21

Almighty God, giver of good gifts, we thank you for parents. We are grateful for their faithfulness and their steadfast hand as they guide, teach and love the children within their care. Give them the wisdom to follow your will and pass along the gifts they have been given; through Jesus Christ our Lord. *Amen*.

In the Session

Discuss: "When to Begin the Conversation" (Chapter 24 in the *These Are Our Bodies: Foundation Book*, page 191). Consider these two questions:

What are some examples of myths that you would have to re-teach your children?

How could you restate them to make them truthful?

What are some of your take aways from your conversations?

Using Correct Terminology

When parents use the correct terminology, concepts do not have to be unlearned or retaught. We want your child to have the basics on which they can build their understanding as they grow.

TIPS AND TERMINOLOGY

Remember to approach the topic in a matter-of-fact way.

Use simple language and clear concepts that will not have to be unlearned. One family taught their child that babies grow in the stomach. When the child learned about the digestive system, she was very confused. Aim to tell your children the truth as best as you can.

Use correct terminology. When parents use the correct terminology, concepts do not have to be unlearned or retaught. You want your children to have the basics on which they can build their understanding as they grow.[8]

....

8 Leslie Choplin and Jenny Beaumont. *These Are Our Bodies: Talking Faith & Sexuality at Church & Home* (New York: Church Publishing, 2016), 192.

Does this resonate for you? If so, how? If not, why?

Would using correct terminology be difficult for you? Why?

ON YOUR OWN

In the next month, think about the terminology that you are using with your children. Consider or practice using standard terms with your child.

> Loving and gracious God, creator and sustainer of all,
> Who knows the challenges and joys of parenting,
> Who made us in the image of the God and calls us
>   "very good,"
> Who gives us a ministry that demands our best efforts,
> Whose presence fills us with gladness,
> We thank you for the community that supports us, for
>   their generous hearts, for their abundant gifts,
>   for their willingness to walk on this journey.
> We thank you for giving us this empowering work.
>   We confess that we may be nervous or anxious.
> Bless us with calm spirits born of your love.
> Bless us with unburdened hearts to listen. Bless us
>   with patience, humor and joy,
> And keep us ever mindful of your love and grace. *Amen*.

WITH YOUR FAMILY AT HOME

You may want to use this activity later to complete this portion of your child's *Participant Book,* found on page 41.

As a family, talk about some words you need to know about the human body. If you want, make a list of about 10 words or terms here that all of you want to learn more about.

Now that you have made a list, talk about those words. Talk about a way to find out information that is factual and true. Ask yourself, where can I find out what a term means? You can add more words later if you want.

SESSION 6

WE ARE
SELF-AWARE

I appeal to you therefore, brothers and sisters, by the mercies of God, to present your bodies as a living sacrifice, holy and acceptable to God, which is your spiritual worship. Do not be conformed to this world, but be transformed by the renewing of your minds, so that you may discern what is the will of God—what is good and acceptable and perfect.

—Romans 12:1–2

O God, you have prepared for those who love you such good things as surpass our understanding: Pour into our hearts such love towards you, that we, loving you in all things and above all things, may obtain your promises, which exceed all that we can desire; through Jesus Christ our Lord, who lives and reigns with you and the Holy Spirit, one God, for ever and ever. *Amen*.[9]

In the Session

The news is filled with pronouncements about modeling healthy body perspectives and images.

As parents raising young children, identify what messages about the human body you want to pass onto your children, and then apply those values into your own life. Many parents want their children to learn that bodies come in many different shapes and sizes, yet talk about a girly, womanly, or manly figure in day-to-day conversations with them.

How can we change our language to model an accepting view of shapes and sizes and orientation?

Another message might be that we are made in the image of God, with diverse and a combination of typically feminine and masculine tendencies. Calling a child wimpy or a tomboy belies our own acceptance of stereotypical views of gender.

Perhaps using gender-neutral adjectives such as gentle, active, sensitive, or sensible would give children a model of openness and acceptance.

Look at the jokes that we tell. When do the topics of our humor belittle others or create joy from at the expense of others? "Your mama is" jokes or "blonde" jokes are seemingly harmless, until we examine the stereotypical attitudes that are being practiced through the guise of humor. Remember that even our subtle comments about others and ourselves can teach. Make note of some of language that you may be using that you might want to change.

Think about the messages that you are giving your children. Take few minutes to consider how you might teach your children about healthy body image.

How could you move further into acceptance and celebration of your body and sexuality?

What might you ask God to help you accept about your body?

How has your view of your body and the human body changed as you have journeyed as a parent?

What are some of the messages that you might give your children about healthy body image?

What does a healthy body image mean to you?

On Your Own

> If anyone is in Christ he is a new creation; the old has passed away, behold the new has come. All this is from God, who through Christ reconciled us to himself and gave us the ministry of reconciliation.
>
> —2 Corinthians 5:17–18

When we judge others or even ourselves, we keep ourselves from becoming the people that we have been intended to be. Teaching our children to live without judgment or evaluation of others and of themselves gives them the grace and space to grow into the people that God has intended them to be.

The constant voice of criticism and appraisal keeps us focused on the opinion of others instead of listening to the wisdom within or the voice of God. My daughter has always loved to sing and dance, sometimes very loudly. It gives her so much joy. In my parenting, I found myself wanting to tamp her down. To ask her to be quieter just didn't resonate with me. I decided to ask myself about the voice I was hearing that was saying, stay small, stay quiet, and stay hidden. In reflecting, I realized that the voice in my head was concerned with what others would think of her or of me. The voice was concerned not with the true self that my daughter was discovering or the best self that God had dreamed for her or that she wanted to be.

That voice was a voice of appraisal and judgment. Once I decided to stop censoring her, to lean into her need to move, sing, and dance, I was able lean into experiencing the joy of her expressing herself. How you move and walk in the world is inherently about a person's sexuality. We can all remember times when our own way of being in the world was criticized or judged and subsequently the pain that was caused in our own lives. As a parent, we strive to lift up our children to give them the space to explore for themselves who they are meant to be.

O God, the protector of all who trust in you, without whom nothing is strong, nothing is holy: Increase and multiply upon us your mercy; that, with you as our ruler and guide, we may so pass through things temporal, that we lose not the things eternal; through Jesus Christ our Lord, who lives and reigns with you and the Holy Spirit, one God, for ever and ever. *Amen*.

Parent Tip: Be comfortable in your skin. One of the best gifts we can give our children is an acceptance of our own body, sexuality, and a sense that we are comfortable in our own skin. Focusing on healthy choices or a balanced approach to food and exercise models freedom to children with some boundaries. Teaching children to make healthy choices in terms of food keeps foods from becoming "outlawed" in the home. Asking how can we add a few more colors to our plate or meals empowers children to practice discernment around their food choices. Focus on exercise as an activity instead of weight or body shape. This helps children to accept their own bodies and their own "imperfections."

SESSION 7

WE ARE LOVING

. . . and that Christ may dwell in your hearts through faith, as
you are being rooted and grounded in love. I pray that you
may have the power to comprehend, with all the saints,
what is the breadth and length and height and depth, and to
know the love of Christ that surpasses knowledge, so that
you may be filled with all the fullness of God. Now to him
who by the power at work within us is able to accomplish
abundantly far more than all we can ask or imagine, to him
be glory in the church and in Christ Jesus to all generations,
forever and ever. *Amen*.

I therefore, the prisoner in the Lord, beg you to lead a life worthy of the calling to which you have been called, with all humility and gentleness, with patience, bearing with one another in love, making every effort to maintain the unity of the Spirit in the bond of peace. There is one body and one Spirit, just as you were called to the one hope of your calling, one Lord, one faith, one baptism, one God and Father of all, who is above all and through all and in all.

—Ephesians 3:17–4:6

Set us free, O God, from the bondage of our sins, and give us the liberty of that abundant life which you have made known to us in your Son our Savior Jesus Christ; who lives and reigns with you, in the unity of the Holy Spirit, one God, now and for ever. *Amen.*[10]

....

10 Book of Common Prayer, 2016

In the Session

Many parents want to teach their children that they are not just their bodies. They are whole people and more than bodies, yes, including their minds and souls. We are connected people. Children not only learn what we talk about, but they also learn from our behavior. Talking about our weight, size, hair growth, or hair loss teaches children that our bodies have some control over us. When parents try on several dresses and ask whether the dresses make them look fat or whether their butt looks too big, we are teaching our children to assess themselves by how their bodies are perceived by others. If you need to try on several things, do it behind closed doors instead of passing along the idea that we don't look good enough. As humans, we naturally assess and judge. Sometimes, maybe this judgement seems harmless, until we realize the damage that it has done. As a parent, think about new ways of giving children compliments that lift up the child instead of focusing on external beauty.

A parent in one of our workshops gave an example that I applied in my own home. She told a story about a father who instead of saying, "That shirt makes you look thin, cute, or pretty," would look up and say, "Wow, you make that shirt look awesome. You really show it off!" The parent felt like the clothes she wore showed off her inner self instead of the clothes being the beautiful part to show the world. She learned confidence from that and an ability to focus on the beauty within. Sending messages around healthy expectations in terms of clothes and bodies continues throughout our parenting. When we are able to articulate a focus on the person and not the body or clothes, children learn to embrace a healthy self-image and learn to be less self-critical.

Let's look at the language that we use around sexuality.

Our conceptions of male and female, family and singleness, orientation and expression can be unintentionally expansive and accepting or confining and judging. Asking if someone has a boyfriend or girlfriend can be gender confining to someone who is not gender conforming. Asking when someone is going to get married or have children can be perceived as invasive, insensitive, or insulting! As a cisgender[11] female, I have tried to replace my social inquires to show interest in other people without pre-defining or assuming their experience or their intentions for the future. Statements have helped to open up conversation in a way that the person can own and define the conversation: Tell me what things you are excited about these days. I would love to hear what you are doing these days. I am excited to catch up with you. Tell me about your family.

Although they can seem awkward at first, those statements leave the control of the conversation with the other person; the other person can choose what they want to share.

As we practice these more open and loving ways of responding to others, we will naturally see ways in which we have failed other in the past.

....

11 Cisgender relates to someone whose personal identity corresponds to their assigned sex at birth.

Remember to forgive yourself and realize that we all have the ability to grow and change.

Perhaps you might need to apologize for past conversations and perhaps your new way of approaching and relating to others will be enough to establish a more loving and aware relationship.

What does an abundant life mean to you?

What does the good life mean?

How might our behavior or language hinder our children from attaining the good life?

What are we teaching our children that they may have to relearn?

On Your Own

Read the following scenario:

When my son was in preschool, he walked into my room early one morning. I was pregnant with our third child. We were talking about mommies and babies. We were also talking about taking turns. My two boys were taking turns talking to the growing baby. He asked, "When can it be my turn to be a girl?" I admit I had not seen this question coming. I just said, "Tell me what made you think of that." His response: "I want to be a girl. Why can't I be a girl?" "Tell me why you want to be a girl." "I want to be a mommy." Oh my. I clearly saw that I had not been lifting up the joy of being a parent . . . only the joy of being a mommy.

My child gave me the opportunity to change the way I talked about families, babies, and parents. We were able to talk about the things that were done to help a family grow and be healthy. Babies needed to be fed, someone needed to work, and someone needed to cook and do yard work.

Talking about roles in a more open way helped us all see that organizing roles in a gender traditional way was not necessary and that sometimes we didn't teach our children the lesson that we would want them to learn.

Reflect on what you have read and journal about your insights.

CHOOSING GENDER AND ROLE NON-CONFORMITY

One afternoon during pickup from preschool, my child's teacher came to the door where I was standing obviously ready to chat. She excitedly blurted out, "I can't believe you let him wear those to school. That is so wonderful. Most parents wouldn't let him wear those."

I clearly was not following the conversation and with a very puzzled look, I asked, "What did he wear to school?" The teacher explained that when they were in the bathroom, my child had asked for help pulling up his pantyhose. I actually didn't know that he had worn them to school, but I did know that he liked to wear pantyhose, as he called them, under his regular clothes. At home he was so proud to be able to put them on and take them off.

He was dressing up in adult clothes, just like children who wear their parent's shoes. I love that story because it showed me that he was comfortable trying out the roles that he saw around him and that he was not constrained by gender norms. The challenge continues as they grow!

The fight around clothes and hairstyles can become contentious as children become older and assert their own sense of style into the picture. Hair is a direct expression of a person's sexuality. Criticism of hairstyles can be particularly hurtful to young people. I remember my first hairstyle, a pixy cut in first grade. I was so excited about my new cut until a couple of neighbors teased me about trying be a boy even with my hair. Being labeled a tomboy quickly ensued.

Remembering that hair can grow back and color eventually wears off, helps us to rethink some of our conforming norms around hair. As my boys grew older and wanted to grow their hair long, I tried to remember the hurt I felt as a young child and decided to embrace and accept their choices instead of evaluating and judging them.

When thinking about gender and nonconformity, what challenges you?

Jesus implores us to relinquish our hold on judgment. "Do not judge" seems to be a constant command. Often we think of the judgment in terms of judging others, but the self-judging can be just as poisonous in our relationships.

Read chapter 6, "A New Way of Understanding our Sexuality" beginning on page 47 in *These Are Our Bodies: Foundation Book*. Reflect on the questions offered on pages 56 and 57.

A Collect for Guidance

Heavenly Father, in you we live and move and have our being: We humbly pray you so to guide and govern us by your Holy Spirit, that in all the cares and occupations of our life we may not forget you, but may remember that we are ever walking in your sight; through Jesus Christ our Lord. *Amen.*[12]

....

12 Book of Common Prayer, 100

SESSION 8

WE ARE
CONSIDERATE

The whole story of creation, incarnation, and our incorporation into the fellowship of Christ's body tells us that God desires us, as if we were God, as if we were that unconditional response to God's giving that God's self makes in the life of the Trinity. We are created so that we may be caught up in this and so that we may grow into the wholehearted love of God by learning that God loves us as God loves God.[13]
—Rowan D. Williams

....

13 Rowan D. Williams. "The Body's Grace" in *Theology and Sexuality: Classic and Contemporary Readings*, ed. Eugene F. Rogers, Jr. (New Jersey: Blackwell Publishing, 2002), 311–312.

Almighty God, Father of all mercies, we thine unworthy servants do give thee most humble and hearty thanks for all thy goodness and loving-kindness to us and to all men. We bless thee for our creation, preservation, and all the blessings of this life; but above all for thine inestimable love in the redemption of the world by our Lord Jesus Christ, for the means of grace, and for the hope of glory. And, we beseech thee, give us that due sense of all thy mercies, that our hearts may be unfeignedly thankful; and that we show forth thy praise, not only with our lips, but in our lives, by giving up our selves to thy service, and by walking before thee in holiness and righteousness all our days; through Jesus Christ our Lord, to whom, with thee and the Holy Ghost, be all honor and glory, world without end. *Amen*.[14]

In the Session

We have all experienced shame—that sense that "I am bad." And have probably even said, "You should be ashamed of yourself." We know that a pattern of shame leads to feeling undeserving of love. As parents, we seek to use everything within our power to lift up and encourage our children.

According to Brené Brown, "Shame is the intensely painful feeling or experience of believing that we are flawed and therefore unworthy of love and belonging."[15]

How have you experienced shaming in your life?

What messages of shame were you given growing up?

....

15 Brené Brown. *Daring Greatly: How the Courage to Be Vulnerable Transforms the Way We Live, Love, Parent, and Lead* (New York: Avery, 2012), 69.

How might shifting our language change our children's sense of worthiness and belonging?

SHAME

Shame is one of the deepest and harmful human emotions. How can we find a new way of language that frees us from shameful language and responses?

Children who feel loved—body and soul—grow up with a sense of worthiness and belonging. Children are a gift to families—and families are charged with bringing up healthy children who have a positive view of sexuality. To foster healthy sexual education at home, families can create loving and supportive relationships while teaching responsibility for self and others and valuing equality in sexual identity, attraction, and expression.

A gentle touch or a hurried, rushed touch teaches either kindness or frustration. The words used at changing time echo in children. When a bowel movement is met with "That is stinky, YUCK!" it teaches a toddler that their bodily functions are inherently revolting and creates a sense of shame.

Parents can substitute empowering words of affirmation and acceptance that can work to create shame resilience in their children. A more affirmative choice would be, "Let's get you cleaned up and more comfortable."

Leaning into the infant or toddler to blow on their stomach playfully demonstrates connection. That intimacy and tenderness says: "You are worthy. You are loved. You are treasured." And those messages of love and acceptance are felt through their bodies; they are the messages of meaning.

SHAME VS. AFFIRMATION EXERCISE

Begin by writing messages of shame. Then change those statements into loving affirmations.

Consider some of the shame filled phrase and their affirming alternatives:

Affirming	Shaming
Your hands are sticky; let's wipe them off.	You are all sticky. Yuck.
Let's share toys.	You are selfish.
Oops! Let's pick this up.	You are clumsy.
Be careful. Try to make your body still.	You are like a bull in a china shop.

On Your Own

Lord Jesus Christ, who didst stretch out thine arms of love on the hard wood of the cross that everyone might come within the reach of thy saving embrace: So clothe us in thy Spirit that we, reaching forth our hands in love, may bring those who do not know thee to the knowledge and love of thee; for the honor of thy Name. *Amen*.[16]

....

16 Book of Common Prayer, 58

With Your Family at Home

You may want to use this activity later to complete this portion of your child's Participant Book, found on pages 44–45.

A loving affirmation makes the heart, mind, and body feel good. Practice writing words that talk about goodness, love, acceptance, and a joy-filled life. Try filling in these blanks with your family. After filling them in with words that say how good something is, try saying them aloud to each other. You could also write them on paper and put them around the house as reminders. Challenge each other to say these kind words as often as you see the reminders.

My body is _____.

Your body is _____.

I love my _____.

I love your _____.

When you are around, I feel _____.

You have great _____.

I have great _____.

My _____ are beautiful.

My _____ is amazing.

SESSION 9

WE TEACH
CONSENT

Don't do anything for selfish purposes, but with humility think
of others as better than yourselves. Instead of each person
watching out for their own good, watch out for what is
better for others.

—Philippians 2:3–4 (CEB)

In the Session

TEACH "NO" AND "STOP"

- Young children are often taught to say, "Yes" to adults. It can be a sign of respect and unfortunately it can also teach children not to questions adults' authority. Empower your children to say, "No" when they need to.

- Using the word "Stop" and listening to the word "Stop" are both important words young children can use to express their needs or wants.

- When it comes to your children's bodies, help them know that they can voice a "Yes" or "No" or "Stop" and that statement will be respected. This can be taught around food or play or even clothing. Let children decide if they want what is being offered. Don't force them to have seconds or just try a bite. Ask for permission to tickle your child. Practice and model the concepts of "No, Stop, Ask" permission and listening to others when they hear "No" or "Stop." Teach that the phrase, "I am not having fun," means "Stop." Respect the rights of others to say, "No" or "Stop."

- Teach children to check in with their friends during playtime to make sure everyone is still having fun. Wrestling and tickling can go from fun to aggression quickly.

ENCOURAGE CHILDREN TO TALK ABOUT THEIR BODIES

- Children who can talk about their bodies are more able to express that their space is being violated. They may not say those words, but they can say, "I feel uncomfortable." And as parents, listen and acknowledge your children whenever they are feeling uncomfortable in a situation or with a person or group.

- Listening to your children's concerns and apprehensions will help to keep the conversation open.

ALLOW CHILDREN TO HAVE CONTROL OVER THEIR OWN BODY

- Don't force children to kiss or hug people on command. Help them learn different ways of greeting.

- It can be awkward at first, but allowing children to choose whether they want to be kissed, hugged, or cuddled will bear fruit in the future as they grow and develop.

- Remember that you are teaching skills that will protect them as they grow older, and you as the parents are not always with them.

MAKE THE PHRASE "BODY AUTONOMY" COMMON IN YOUR HOME.

- "Body autonomy" means that you are the one who gets to decide what you do with your body.

- It means other people will respect our right to decide if we want to hug or wrestle.

- It means that we will respect other people's right to decide if they want to hug or wrestle.

How can you introduce the concept of body autonomy in your home?

On Your Own

T.E.A.M.

Teach that "No" means "No."
Encourage children to talk about their bodies.
Allow children to have control over their own body.
Make the phrase "body autonomy" common in your home.

Read chapter 9, "Consent and Shame" beginning on page 75 in *These Are Our Bodies: Foundation Book*.

Almighty God, Father of all mercies, we your unworthy servants give you humble thanks for all your goodness and loving-kindness to us and to all whom you have made. We bless you for our creation, preservation, and all the blessings of this life; but above all for your immeasurable love in the redemption of the world by our Lord Jesus Christ; for the means of grace, and for the hope of glory. And, we pray, give us such an awareness of your mercies, that with truly thankful hearts we may show forth your praise, not only with our lips, but in our lives, by giving up our selves to your service, and by walking before you in holiness and righteousness all our days; through Jesus Christ our Lord, to whom, with you and the Holy Spirit, be honor and glory throughout all ages. *Amen.*[16]

With Your Family at Home

You may want to use this activity later to complete this portion of your child's Participant Book, found on pages 46–47.

Using the following secret code, uncover with your parents a phrase you need to know. (Answer: BODY AUTONOMY)

A = 20	H = 11	O = 25	V = 22
B = 15	I = 17	P = 16	W = 19
C = 1	J = 21	Q = 12	X = 10
D = 3	K = 13	R = 26	Y = 24
E = 14	L = 5	S = 8	Z = 4
F = 6	M = 2	T = 23	
G = 9	N = 18	U = 7	

....
15   25   3   24

....
20   7   23   25   18   25   2   24

With your child, talk about what you discovered. What does it mean? Why is it important?

RESOURCES

Authors' note to parents:
These Are Our Bodies: Foundation Book has an extensive glossary, bibliography, and overview of child development that we recommend for your own information as well as to support and understand your child.

Organizations
- **Advocates for Youth:** Helps young people make informed and responsible decisions about their reproductive and sexual health; offers lessons and curricula. www.advocatesforyouth.org/sex-education-home
- **The Center for Lesbian & Gay Studies in Religion and Ministry:** Has a mission to advance the well-being of lesbian, gay, bisexual, queer, and transgender people and to transform faith communities and the wider society by taking a leading role in shaping a new public discourse on religion, gender identity, and sexuality through education, research, community building, and advocacy. http://clgs.org
- **The Coalition for Positive Sexuality:** Offers information in English and Spanish for young people who are sexually active or considering sexual activity. http://positive.org

- **Common Sense Media:** A trusted media education resources offers questions and answers regarding privacy and the internet. www.commonsensemedia.org/privacy-and-internet-safety
- **Faith Trust Institute:** A national, multi-faith, multicultural training and education organization that works to end sexual and domestic violence. www.faithtrustinstitute.org
- **Integrity USA:** An organization "proclaiming God's inclusive love in and through the Episcopal Church since 1975." www.integrityusa.org
- **Religious Institute:** A multi-faith organization dedicated to advocating for sexual health, education, and justice in faith communities and societies. www.religiousinstitute.org
- **Stop Bullying:** Information, videos, lessons, and more to respond to bullying. www.stopbullying.gov
- **Trans Student Educational Resources:** A youth-led organization dedicated to transforming the educational environment for trans and gender nonconforming students through advocacy and empowerment. In addition to creating a more trans-friendly education system, their mission is to educate the public and teach trans activists how to be effective organizers. TSER believes that justice for trans and gender nonconforming youth is contingent on an intersectional framework of activism. Ending oppression is a long-term process that can only be achieved through collaborative action. www.transstudent.org

Print resources

- Laura Berman. *Talking to Your Kids About Sex: Turning "The Talk" into a Conversation for Life*. New York: DK Publishing, 2009.
- Stephanie Brill and Pepper, Rachel. *The Transgender Child: A Handbook for Families and Professionals.* San Francisco, CA: Cleis Press, Inc., 2008.
- Robert C. Dykstra, Allan Hugh Cole Jr., and Donald Capps. *Losers, Loners, and Rebels: The Spiritual Struggles of Boys*. Louisville: Westminster John Knox Press, 2007.
- Robie H. Harris. *It's Not the Stork!: A Book About Girls, Boys, Babies, Bodies, Families and Friends*. Somerville, MA: Candlewick Press, 2008.
- Robie H. Harris. *It's So Amazing!: A Book about Eggs, Sperm, Birth, Babies, and Families*. Somerville, MA: Candlewick Press, 2014.